"Craig's book is a clear, [ ] for the church to be the church!"

-Rick Warren
Senior Pastor, Saddleback Church
Author, *The Purpose Driven Life*

"Craig Strickland is a bridge-building leader who can't stop himself from reaching across chasms of all kinds. My prayer is that every person who reads this book would catch the wonderful disease that has so infected Craig."

-Bill Hybels
Senior Pastor of Willow Creek Community Church and Chairman of the Board of Directors of Willow Creek Association

"My personal mission is to be involved in things that have potential for the 100X impact articulated in the parable of the sower. That is why I am pleased to endorse *Rethinking Reason*. In his new book, Craig casts a vision and speaks with authority as someone who is leading ministry that engages the community and is reaping exponential impact."

-Bob Buford
Founder, Leadership Network
Author, *Halftime* and *Finishing Well*

"Craig Strickland is one of the most unique ministers I know. That's a compliment. He personifies a new brand of pastor-leader who is not as much concerned about doctrinal and denominational identity as he is about modeling servant leadership and developing a servant people. Reading this book, lay and clergy alike will be challenged to rethink reason. The challenge may be painful, but it may also be transformational."

-Maxie Dunnam
Chancellor
Asbury Theological Seminary

"Craig is a visionary, innovator, out-of-the-box thinker and is in concert with the true mandate and mission of Christ. He is color-blind and unconditionally committed to serving others. One of life's greatest joys is finding God's purpose for your life and following it. Craig Strickland is in his 'sweet spot' as a modern-day church leader... he is also a personal hero of mine."

-Kemmons Wilson, Jr.
Principal
Kemmons Wilson Companies

"If a person is known as much by the questions they ask as by their answers, then you're going to love this account of one man's pilgrimage of discovery and faith. Especially if you, like him, are just an ordinary human being seeking someone to fill an awful void. If you are fed up with religion this book is for you. This is not about religion; this is about life."

-Bill Pannell
Senior Professor of Preaching and Special Assistant to
the President Fuller Theological Seminary

rethinking | **reason**

rethinking | **reason**

with so many different faiths, does someone
have to be wrong for someone to be right?

r. craig strickland

TATE PUBLISHING & *Enterprises*

Published by Tate Publishing & Enterprises, LLC
127 E. Trade Center Terrace | Mustang, Oklahoma 73064 USA
1.888.361.9473 | www.tatepublishing.com

Tate Publishing is committed to excellence in the publishing industry. The company reflects the philosophy established by the founders, based on Psalm 68:11,
"The Lord gave the word and great was the company of those who published it."

Book design copyright © 2007 by Tate Publishing, LLC. All rights reserved.
Cover design by Jack Kelley
Interior design by Jacob Crissup

Published in the United States of America

ISBN: 978-1-60462-446-5
1. Religion: Christianity   2. Christian Life: Social Issues
07.11.09

dedication

To the greatest servant leader I have ever known—my gracious and loving wife, Lee. She would follow me off the face of the earth without hesitation and yet has always been the most honest critic when I most needed honesty. I wish all the world knew your kind spirit as well as I do. Thanks for sticking with me through the mountains and valleys of life. You're the best. I dedicate this book to you!

acknowledgement

I could not imagine writing a book like this one without having lived in community with the many friends I've made at Hope Church. I have learned more from them than I would have ever possibly imagined. If you happen to be one who has grown to love the Hope Family like I have, thanks for teaching me most of what I know! It has been a humble joy to serve you these last twenty years. I will always remain in your debt.

Various friends have helped me organize my thoughts as I've tried to communicate what I think are the most important truths in the world. Unfortunately, I write like I speak, which takes lots of editing! Bob Russell and Sally Griffin have been relentless in their effort to get this book published. Bob simply doesn't take "no" for an answer, and I never praise him adequately for this incredible gift God has given him. Eli Morris has served by my side for twenty years. I wouldn't be the man I am today apart from his ministry to me. Mike Sadler, Kathy Flake, and Darlene Whitfield have all made many contributions to the early drafts of this manuscript. Mack Oates has modeled for us all the message I have tried to convey in this book. His example has been inspiring. Jack Kelley is the best graphic designer that I know, and he is responsible for the fantastic artwork of this book. My dear friend and mentor, John Richard deWitt, offered to help me from the very beginning. Not only has he shaped my life by teaching me by his own example what a servant-pastor looks like; Dick has continued to shape my thinking through the journey of writing this book. There is no one whose opinion I value as much as his.

My mother and father, who mean the world to me, believed in me long before anyone else and have quietly and faithfully served me and followed my leadership as their pastor since the beginning of Hope Church almost twenty years ago. Thanks always for your encouragement.

All three of our children, Emily, Taylor, and Tucker, have endured the challenges and hardships of being "PK's" and have found times and ways to encourage me when few others knew I needed it most. You all sacrificed your young lives for me to realize God's vision for my life without any choice. There is no more noble cause in my mind. I love and cherish each of you with a father's love. I'm proud to be your father.

table of contents

I'm Pretty Much like You   15

This is not a Book about Joining Something   27

Old Traditions are Fading—People are Ready   45
for a New Thing

Does My Life Really Count?   53

You Don't Shoot Your Wounded   65

You Can Do More Together Than Alone   75

Ali's Way: It Could Be Your Way, Too   87

Tales from the Street   95

Endnotes   101

i'm pretty much like you

I'll go ahead and admit it: my greatest weakness, my greatest sin, is driving too fast—way too fast. At least this is the only sin I'm willing to admit to you. We don't know each other that well. Maybe a little later, when we know each other better, I'll tell you some of my darker weaknesses. They're secret and I don't share them with just anyone—we'll have to become better acquainted. But I do love to drive fast. I heard a guy say the other day that when he gets pulled over by the cops, he just says, "Give me the ticket or the lecture. I'm in a hurry." I bet he usually gets the ticket. Not me—I'll let him scream his head off at me all day long. Just don't give me the ticket. I've learned to be *very* respectful of cops. In a weird way, sometimes I think they may have too much power. But even so, I still drive fast.

I don't really think I'm all that different from you. Maybe your greatest sin isn't driving too fast. Maybe it's drinking too much, or secretly looking at pornography, or looking at other women way too much (I guess if you're married, your wife would say *any* looking is way too much), or maybe it's men, or maybe you've got some other hidden secret you're not willing to tell anybody about. I think pretty much all people have some secret weakness they're not willing to show to the world. We like looking good, and you can't look good if your stuff is hanging out there for the world to see. We go speeding down the road of life hoping we don't get pulled over. Even if we do, just give us the lecture or the ticket. But whatever you do, don't make us look deep inside and ask *why* we were driving too fast.

Other than the stuff I'm not willing to tell you about, as I say, I bet we're not all that different. I'm just an average guy. I went to public high school. I worked at the Sky-Vue Drive-In. Eventually I went off to college and got married. Maybe we can talk more about all of that later. But there's really nothing all that special about me. There is nothing dramatic or flamboyant about me. I'm not well known outside of my own little circle of friends—certainly not outside my own home town. I haven't written a bunch of books.

Sometimes I envy all the pretty people who have lots of fame, or have to avoid the big crowds that follow them, or people with lots of money, or people that seem to live so much better than I do.

I'm pretty much just your average guy. I've spent a lifetime trying to fill the void in my life. I've always wanted to believe that there is something out there for me to do that is bigger than I can imagine. I've tried a lot of stuff, but I'm never completely satisfied with my life. I'm always thinking there is something more.

When I was a teenager, I used to watch my older sister. She always seemed so much more satisfied with her life than I was with mine. She married a great guy, and they seemed to live life with purpose and meaning. They always appeared to have such a keen sense of direction for their lives, even if they didn't always have a lot of money or a nice car or a beautiful new home. Unlike them, I lived life with this hole in my soul. It was like a vacuum that sucked the good feelings right out of me—feelings of wholeness and contentment and worthiness, or the feeling that I knew where my life was headed. I didn't have a clue, so I threw everything I could think of into the hole: everything from alcohol to money and everything in between. It all just got sucked into that black hole. Eventually, I figured out that the black hole was a God-shaped void; the only thing that would fill it up was God. That was my first conscious awareness of the possibility that there might just be something out there bigger than me. There might be something bigger than anything I could imagine. I discovered a Higher Power. Call Him whatever you want. I call him Jesus Christ. I discovered a God who wanted to know me, personally, through his son.

For me, it really wasn't about religion. It was about a relationship—a divine relationship—with the God who created me. I had tried religion and I tried several different kinds of churches, but nothing ever made quite as much sense as this personal relationship with the Creator of the Universe. It was hard for me to imagine that He wanted to know me. I thought He just wanted me to go to church. I really had reinterpreted something Jesus said one time. He said that real worshippers didn't worship in coat and tie, or with stained-glass windows, or in expensive buildings, but simply in spirit and in truth (John 4:21–24). I had not realized that. But when I figured it out,

I discovered there *was* more to life than working at the Sky-Vue Drive-In. God actually wanted me to live fully, abundantly (John 10:10).

Fast forward many years and I discovered that lots and lots of people want to believe there is more to life than they are experiencing: men getting up, eating breakfast, going to a relatively thankless job, coming home, eating dinner in front of the TV, and going to bed; women who feel like they've spent a lifetime picking up dirty socks, doing laundry, cooking a meal that nobody seems all that thankful for no matter what they say in their prayer, doing somebody else's homework, and *maybe* finding a few minutes of intimacy with their husbands.

Now, I know not everybody lives that way. But far more of us live that way than we're ready to admit. We're driving a hundred miles an hour through life just like I do in my car, hoping not to get pulled over. Give us the lecture or the ticket; just don't get into our business. Don't ask us *why* we're driving like there's no tomorrow. We don't want to be found out because in the midst of all our busyness, there are secrets we hope nobody will discover.

We're really not all that happy with our marriage. Deep down inside, we wonder if our kids will ever be as smart as the kids next door, or as pretty or as skilled on a basketball court. We're wishing our little girl were a cheerleader. We're wishing our son were the captain of the football team or the starting center for his high school basketball team or first string pitcher on his high school baseball team, destined for the pros. Maybe deep down inside, where nobody can see, there's this black hole that we're throwing stuff into as fast as we can earn it: new cars, more money, bigger houses, memberships at clubs, new women (or men), or more sexual adventure. Deep down where no one can see we want more power and more prestige. We know we could do our boss's job better than our boss can. If we just made a little more money we could take care of so many problems that keep the pressure on our marriages. Deep down we're ready for change: a new direction in life, a new venue, a new spouse, a new city, a new "look"...*something*...*anything*...to fill the void. But it's a God-shaped vacuum that only He can fill.

What in the world am I here for? I mean *really*?

Back in 1988 I started all over. For me it was like a new career. Although I had been a pastor for ten years (I'm reluctant to tell you that just yet because I don't want you to put the book down. Stay with me here...), I was ready to believe there was more to life than I was experiencing, so I started a church. Now remember, I'm a pretty average guy. Back then, not a whole lot of people knew much about planting churches. I sure didn't. So I went to a conference, read a few books, and started out. Even though there was a mother church that paid my salary for awhile, I gave up about the most secure job a guy could have to do something that fails eight out of ten times. It's as risky as crab fishing in Alaska. But maybe not as dangerous. It usually doesn't kill you to fail, but it sure can ruin your life. I've watched a lot of guys fail at church planting and end up in a completely different career. And so I was scared... well, I was scared to death. I used to get up in the middle of the night and pace the floor, asking myself, "You uprooted your family, moved across town, and sold your house to do something most people fail at eight out of ten times—*what were you thinking?*"

I really wanted to believe there was more to life than

what I had been experiencing, so I talked some friends into helping. We borrowed the basement of the mother church, and called 35,000 random people to ask two questions: "Are you an active member of a local church? And, if not, would you like to come to ours?" You see, I figured there were already enough churches for churchgoing people, but for whatever reason, the research showed there were still 150,000 people in our community who weren't going to *any* church. That's the group we targeted: people who had given up on church; people who said, "I don't like church. I quit going to church. For me, church is irrelevant." These were not necessarily people who had given up on God, but for sure, they were people who had given up on church.

So, from the seed of a dream that began with two other couples, my wife, Lee, and I started a little core group of about twenty-five people. We held our first services in the back room of a local restaurant. Our nursery was in the bar, and we rented a daycare center down the street for older kids while teenagers met in the little office suite we rented near the restaurant. On a good day there might have been one hundred and fifty of us...not counting the babies in the bar. The back room smelled like stale beer; and at 11:30, right about the time I stood up to preach, the cooks started banging the pots and pans. After about a year we rented space from a local high school, and we continued to rent their facilities for about six years. That little group of one hundred and fifty slowly grew to about three hundred. It took seven years. I saw guys in other parts of the country with huge, fast growing churches they had started, and I couldn't understand why that wasn't happening for me. I guess that's when I first admitted to myself that I was really just an average guy. I admitted that I'm really not that different from you. In fact, I pretty much gave up on anything happening on a grand scale in my life. After all, I went to public school and finished graduate school in the dead middle of my class, at best.

It was around that time that this little group of people inspired me to believe that maybe there was something going on in our lives that was greater than ourselves...if we were just willing to believe it. We bought some land for a new church, which was about five times as much land as most new churches normally purchase. This was the first sign that we actually were willing to believe God might do something great in our lives. We built the first little building, again scared to death that no one would come, that we'd be stuck with this huge note we couldn't afford to pay, and that the bank would come after us individually. That's when God did something big...scary big. Eight hundred people came to the opening service, and they kept coming back. And this new church we called Hope became one of the fastest growing churches in the country. That's when it hit me: God is about something much bigger than me.

Now, I'm going to tell you it's real easy to get prideful. Arrogance is way up there at the top of the list of things I'm not yet willing to tell you about, but when you start something, and it begins to grow and grow and grow, it's really easy to start thinking that it's all about you. You start thinking that maybe you are the cause of the growth. It's your great leadership. It's your great public-speaking ability. It's your terrific personality. Maybe, just maybe, you are one of the *chosen* ones. Maybe you are destined to be rich and famous, or at least famous and certainly rich by the world's standards; and by anyone's standards, successful. In fact, most of the guys I went to seminary with would give their right arms to pastor one of the fastest growing churches in the country.

But suddenly right in the middle of my self-imposed journey to greatness, Lee was diagnosed with cancer. Just about the time I began to feel like I had done something great (we all tend to take credit when things go great and blame God when things don't, would you not agree?), life, as we knew it, suddenly changed. Our world was turned upside down. With three kids in high school, suddenly the care-giver became the care-receiver. We sat down at the dining-room table one afternoon and I said, "All of these years, Mom has taken care of us. Now it's time for us to take care of her. We can't take her cancer away, but we sure can take care of her while she battles it. The only way we'll get through this is as a team." And so our oldest, Emily, did the laundry, made dinner, cleaned house, and generally took over as Mom. And Taylor and Tucker, the twins, fed the dogs. Don't laugh! That was a big responsibility for them in those days. Today they both work in global missions—in Ecuador, Iraq, and Mexico. Soon their borders will extend to Honduras, Argentina and further. Now, they feed everybody's dogs.

It was a year to remember. For us as a family, it was a benchmark year. Emily remembers what she calls a Hallmark moment. I was mad at her for not helping out when we needed her most and she said, "You can accuse me of a lot of things, but don't accuse me of not loving my family!"

It was a fork in the road. I could continue to fight with her or I could stop. I said, "Emily, I didn't mean to accuse you of not loving your family." I gave her a big hug and she gave me a bigger hug back. That's when the daughter became the caregiver for the father. She said, "Daddy, don't worry. Mom is going to be okay. Whatever happens, she's in God's hands." And she was right.

I quit going to work every day that year. I moved my office home so I could be close to Lee. The leadership of the church understood. I preached on the weekends and took care of Lee during the week. I never missed a doctor's appointment. I learned to wash her hair and change her bandages and empty the little plastic drainage bags attached to her body. I learned what it meant to receive love from others.

And I learned what it meant to give love to Lee. It might have been the first time I began to realize on a personal level the power of servant-leadership. I thought I was just fulfilling a vow I made when we got married: "For better or for worse, for richer or for poorer, in sickness and in health, forsaking all others, as long as we both shall live."

Most days when we came home from the hospital there were five meals in the kitchen. There was so much food that year; we still had meals in the freezer two years later. Every morning someone would leave freshly baked bread and breakfast pastries at our kitchen door. We'd just open the door and there they would be. Lee still cherishes a box of notes that she keeps on a closet shelf that were given by well wishers. Many of them are notes from people she doesn't even know. And those notes, in their own way, taught us what it means to serve others.

We learned to talk about the really important things in life. I can still remember a particular place we would drive by on the way to chemotherapy where Lee would open up and talk about the profound desires of her heart. She wanted to see a daughter walk down the aisle at her wedding, watch her boys graduate from high school, and hold a newborn grandchild.

Lee got well, and once more I realized that there was something bigger in life than I could imagine. I also realized that the most important thing to me wasn't being the pastor of a big church. The most important thing to me was being a good husband to Lee and a good dad to Emily, Taylor and Tucker and today a good grandfather to Scottie and West.

There is so much more to life than I ever imagined. Jesus Christ once said, "I have come that they may have life, and have it to the full" (John 10:10b). When I finally decided to start trusting God with the details of my life I discovered some of the good living, the abundant life the Bible talks about. Not all of it felt so good, but it sure was fulfilling. It was greater than anything I could have imagined—even the bad. It really wasn't all that dramatic or flamboyant at the time, but I began to realize back then at some point what in the world I was here for.

Okay, Let's Review:

1. What's your secret sin?

2. What voids are you trying to fill in your life? How?

3. If you could contribute one thing *right now* to the world, what would it be?

4. Describe what the perfect community of faith would look like to you. Now Google it and plan a trip there.

5. How does pride keep you from accepting others who are different than you? How can you change that?

6. How has your worst nightmare made you become a better person?

7. Is there somebody in trouble you know *right now?* What action could you take *today* or *tomorrow* that would make them feel loved?

Don't wait. Just do it.

this is not a book about joining something

This is not a book about joining something. Nor about criticizing what somebody else might be doing. It's not a book against something.

As I get older I'm starting to realize that all the strong convictions I've held in life, all the doctrine I've fought for, all the "enemies" I've conjured up may not be going to Hell after all. Don't get me wrong. I haven't compromised my belief system. I still hold the tenets of my faith very close to my heart. I'm just willing to admit that all I know may not be totally right at the end of the day.

I know a group that defines itself by who they are not. They are not fallible, broken, sometimes mistaken human beings. They hold The Truth. So help their God, they hold The Truth. I don't think it has dawned on them that they could be wrong. Or at least not as right as they think they are. And so they prowl around looking for someone else to attack, someone to be against, someone who doesn't measure up to their standards. Arguably, they have some pretty high standards. I certainly wouldn't measure up. They have drawn a pretty tight circle, and those who "fit" within the circle are the "righteous," the "faithful remnant," those who are "Holier than Thou." It's fine with me that such a group exists. But I'm afraid that they've created a standard that's pretty hard to live up to. And it looks just great until somebody falls. And one day each member *will* fall. And eventually there won't be anyone in the group. Because we all fall.

I have a very close friend who used to be a cop. Now he helps cops pick up the pieces after they've been through a critical incident, like a shooting or stabbing, or the death of an officer in the line of duty, that sort of thing. He is very, very good at what he does. He heals cops. Only a cop understands just how important it is that somebody be there for them. But my friend Pete is there for them. Period. Night or day, 24/7. He is on call 24 hours a day 365 days a week. And he's a remarkable man. I've never seen a group of law enforcement officers who are lied to and disrespected every day—who develop a very thick shell of self-defense—willing to trust a man as quickly and genuinely as they trust Pete. When I met Pete, he didn't like me much. He knew too many guys like me. They weren't people—they were pastors or priests. Does that make sense? In other words, they lived this role; they played this part of a "God-person." A person who represented God. A Holy Man. You couldn't see their flaws. They wore an impenetrable armor through which they thought others couldn't see. But Pete was no fool. Like most people, he could see through the façade. He saw the chinks in the armor. And he knew, deep down, that they too had their struggles, their doubts. They just didn't talk about them. He had seen too much graft and corruption in the church. He had seen too many clergy and too many church people who walked one way and talked another. So when I met Pete, he still loved to hate clergy guys like me—he thought we were a bunch of know-it-alls who were about as bogus as people come.

I'm guessing it took me six months to convince Pete I wasn't like the pastors or priests he grew up with in South Boston. It was no big deal. I did it by serving cops. I have been the chaplain for three law enforcement agencies for several years. It's no game for me. I genuinely wanted to help others. And I have this unique role with law enforcement. In addition to riding along with cops and getting to know them, I also make death notifications for them. It's probably the thing cops least like to do. So it is something I do that I think makes a real difference for cops and for people who have to receive horrifically tragic news.

When Hurricane Katrina hit the Gulf Coast, it was a nightmare for all people—cops included. There were cops patrolling Mississippi Gulf Coast towns in their flip-flops. They had no house; they were living in the cars they were driving. They had nothing, but they were still doing their job—often working eighteen-hour shifts or even longer. And a group of friends from Hope came along side law enforcement officers in Tennessee and provided all the resources government couldn't provide: food, clothing, household items, incidentals, whatever. We were there. I really didn't think it was any big deal. We were being what I call "The Body of Christ" for a group of people who desperately needed some help. We were there. Every week they needed us. Almost three months, every week. When

Pete saw Hope people "walking their talk" he changed his mind about Hope and about me.

Pete once told me that he sat out in the parking lot of the church late one afternoon and watched people coming in and going out. He said, "I couldn't understand it. They all seemed to have smiles on their faces. I had never seen people smile so much. I kept wondering what they had to be so happy about." What my friend saw was the beauty, the magic, of people helping people, people *loving their neighbor*. I read that somewhere (Leviticus 19:18 ASV). And again, the influence just expands. It's just people serving people. When people serve people, remarkable things happen.

When I was a kid everybody loathed the Communists. We had an enemy to despise…to fear. Then the Iron Curtain fell. And the Cold War warmed up. And we found ourselves without a worthy adversary to defend ourselves against. So we simply continued to fight each other. We really had never stopped. Racism was rampant. But over time, racism went underground. It didn't go away; it just went underground. One could be Black, or White, or Latino, or Asian, but if they are illegal immigrants, we don't like them. But even with our own internal disagreements as a nation, it didn't take long for us to find someone with whom we could vehemently disagree. I hope you're not from the Middle East—or an illegal immigrant. Because once again, we've found someone we love to hate. Or at least distrust. An adversary, an opponent, an antagonist. And if you happen to be one of those people, you just made our short list. Because as much as we may hate to admit it, *loving thy neighbor* doesn't come all that easy, even when he or she lives in your own back yard.

When I went to graduate school, I was taught to think and believe a certain way. And I was taught that my way was the right way. What my professors believed was correct, and the only belief system worth trusting. I'm all about strong convictions. In fact, I have lived my entire adult life in the Evangelical Christian camp. To take it a bit further, I've lived in the smaller camp with the Presbyterians. The Conservative Evangelical Presbyterians. And I've even fallen into the trap of drawing a very tight circle around myself. I'm a five-point Calvinist. Now, it really doesn't matter if you know what a five-point Calvinist is. Calvinism and Arminianism—two words that have divided entire branches of Christianity. We've divided the Catholics from the Protestants, and then we divided the Protestants into hundreds of smaller denominations. And yet even with all the dividing, no one can seem to agree on exactly *who* holds the corner on truth.

A few years ago I learned that maybe the world is changing. But we're like the frog in the kettle full of water that slowly warms up without the frog's notice until the frog eventually boils in his own juice and never even knows it until its too late. And the sad truth is, the leaders may be the problem. I have no idea if you could really do that with a frog, but it sure makes a good illustration. Maybe pastors and leaders of various other religious groups are the problem. Do you ever have those thoughts?

A few years ago I got a letter from a local Methodist pastor in town. The letter, which looked like a form letter, said that his new little church plant had exhausted all of its church and denominational resources and was sending a letter to fifty leaders in the community hoping each would give $7,000 so they could build their first building on land they had already purchased and were working hard to pay for. I didn't know the pastor personally but our church is pretty open-minded; so I sent the letter to the Missions Committee. This is just a small group of staff and members who decide where we spend the meager missions dollars we collect from our congregation's gifts and offerings. I expected there would be a healthy discussion about the letter; maybe even for a couple of hours (committees love to discuss stuff), and then they would probably decide to give the $7,000. I couldn't tell, but maybe there would even be a split vote from the committee—some in favor, some opposed. Boy was I surprised when the committee immediately and with no discussion gave the money away. I was even more surprised when I learned that the local newspaper wanted to write a story about it. And even more stunned when I told the congregation (I wanted them to know before the article came out in the newspaper) and they applauded at each service! A Presbyterian Church gave money to a Methodist Church? *Why in the world* would that be newsworthy? Isn't the Church *supposed* to help those in need? Well yeah, as long as it's not the competition. How did we get to thinking other churches were the competition, the adversary, the foe, the rival? I thought the enemy was supposed to be the Enemy...Satan? That's what we learned in seminary. But we sure didn't learn to give our money to the Methodists!

That's when it hit me: the people aren't the problem; the leaders are the problem. We've grown a world full of egocentric leaders in the church, in business, in government; pretty much everywhere. And here I was, right in the middle of the problem. Not out of the blue...but smack dab in the *middle* of the blue. And so I decided there must be something going on in the world that was not only bigger than I was but bigger than the small circle I had drawn around me. I began to see that the world, or at least some of the world, might be changing. Maybe it wasn't about the Kingdom of Craig or even the Kingdom of Hope (our church)…but maybe, just maybe, it was about the Kingdom of God. But I'll tell you, people, especially leaders, catch on real slowly. Most pastors I knew weren't willing to think, or to *let their people think*, outside the box.

I wanted to know what other pastors were thinking, so I started a lunch for pastors. I invited all the pastors I knew to come. I said, "We'll share how our church grew so fast, we'll share our successes and our failures, *and* we'll feed you a free lunch." I thought a group of a half a dozen pastors would come, but within a year there were about one hundred pastors and church leaders: men and women of all denominations, Black and White and Hispanic and Asian. It was the only truly diverse group I have known about in the city for my thirty years of active ministry. And we met every month. I don't know if it was the food or the subject or the friendships or all of that, but the group is still meeting today. We meet every month. We enjoy a free lunch, a good time, and a practical message. Today, this has evolved into a network where lots of different leaders teach about a lot of different subjects. But we insist that the teaching is always practical and always real. No bragging. No boasting. Just real. This group, this network of pastors, has caused me to rethink my formal training. These people weren't my adversaries, my competition. They quickly became my friends.

I tend to learn the hard way. One of those pastors

invited me to have a cup of coffee sometime. Although I quickly agreed, a year later I hadn't bothered to take him up on his invitation. Something happened that reminded me of his offer and guiltily I called him and invited him to have lunch.

Over lunch I said, "Fred, about a year ago you invited me to have a cup of coffee. If I'm not mistaken, what you were really asking me to do is pursue a friendship. I didn't do it. I don't really have an excuse. I could make something up but I'd be lying. I just didn't do it. I'm busy, but I'm no busier than you are. I just didn't do it. And I'm sorry. Would you be willing to forgive me? Could we start all over?"

Now this guy lived *two doors down from me* at the time! I saw him cutting his grass, working in his yard, coming and going, but I couldn't find time for a cup of coffee!

He could not have been more gracious. Fred said, "Sure, no need to even ask. All is forgiven."

Then later during lunch he invited me to go with him and his wife on a missions trip to Zambia. Our church had been doing some missions work in Kenya, but I'd never been to Zambia. I had no plans to go to Zambia. But a network is not a network, a friendship is not a friendship, unless it goes in both directions. So I said, "Let me see what I can do. I'll have to find the money and we've never done anything in Zambia, but let me see. I'll call you."

He told me later that he never expected to hear from me. I went back to the Church and found the money to go with him to Zambia. Because a network is not a network, a friendship is not a friendship, unless it flows both ways. When I went to Zambia, I learned some pretty important lessons. I discovered that my charismatic friend knew far more about missions than anybody in our church. His staff had developed a sophisticated strategy of accountability that was way over my head. And more importantly, we became fast friends.

A couple of years ago the Tsunami hit. Hope Church felt compelled, as a community of faith, to collect an offering to distribute to those whose lives were devastated by this tragic disaster. Only then did I realize we really had no way of distributing the money. We had no contacts in the devastated areas. But my charismatic friend Fred, who pastored a church so different in theology and doctrine from my own, had been working with twenty churches in Sri Lanka for years.

I called Fred and said, "We've collected some money for these people who were hurt so badly by the Tsunami, but we don't really have a good vehicle to distribute the money. I know you're going to Sri Lanka in a couple of weeks, would you mind if we sent some money with you?"

He said, "I wouldn't mind at all." So I met Fred at Starbucks and gave him a check for one hundred and twenty thousand dollars. When Fred saw the check he stuttered, "Am I reading this right or did they put too many zeros on the check?"

I said, "No, you've got it right."

He said, "I'm flabbergasted! A Presbyterian Church writing a check to an Independent Charismatic Church? You *are* going with us? You *are* going to oversee the expenditure of the money, aren't you?"

I said, "No, why would I want to do that? I'm busy with several projects at Hope. I can't go. Besides, Fred, I trust you. I've been with you when you've spent mission's dollars. You do a better job than we do. I know it will go to the people that need it the most."

Because Fred reached out to me and I finally reached back, he's become one of my very dear friends. In fact, he now directs this network of pastors and I come and help him.

You see, I've learned from my own people at Hope that there's something bigger going on in the world than us. It's not about *our* Kingdom. It's about the Kingdom of God. And if we seek His Kingdom, there is no need for us to worry about what may happen to us, because He will take care of the rest of the details (Matthew 6:25–34). And by the way, I'm not a pastor of *authority* in that pastor's network. I'm a pastor of *influence*. I don't have the authority to tell anyone in that group what to do. If they follow my leadership it's because they *want* to, not because they *have* to. And sometimes I follow their leadership. I like it that way. It goes against the grain of what I was taught, but I have learned more from the men and women in the network than I've learned since my days in graduate school over thirty years ago.

Too often we tend to focus our attention, our energy, and our resources on the needs in our tiny little circles; and when we do, we miss the larger things God is doing in the world. Sometimes we make a financial commitment to a missionary or a mission's agency that represents the very small circle we live in. Years go by and no one stops to ask the question, "Is there any evidence that the money we've spent here has made a tangible difference?" Sometimes we discover that multiple churches from multiple denominations have been giving money to the same needy area for years, but they have not stopped to consider the cost of doing ministry alone or the value of joining hands to do ministry together. Not only could valuable ministry resources be expended more efficiently, but people of different color and faith could work side by side, strengthening friendships with people from their own hometowns while building new friendships with new friends in developing, needy cities and countries.

For many years the American Church has sent money and missionaries to developing countries with little if any accountability, rarely if ever joining with other groups who are going to the same places trying to accomplish many of the same things. The results are often an entitlement mentality where churches in developing countries are interested in money but little else. Who can blame them? We've spent a generation teaching them to expect it. It reminds me of the guy who goes door to door in his neighborhood everyday giving away twenty dollar bills. He does it every day for a week. The next week at the appointed time, people started opening their doors and asking, "Hey, where's my twenty dollars?" The man never said he was making a career of giving away twenty dollar bills. But in only a week's time, people came to expect the money. I have been to many countries where good, faithful, godly people welcome me with open arms and ask innocently, "Where's our money?" We have taught them to expect it. Coming along side people and churches and teaching them to be self-sufficient, teaching them to "fish," is much more strategic than handing them money or giving them "fish." In this way, everyone grows.

Last year I had one of the most gratifying experiences of my life. I was asked to participate in a city-wide concert called "Tearing Down the Walls." It was a mix of music, drama, and message of reconciliation led by the leading Jewish contemporary singer/songwriter Rick Recht, and joined by Micah Greenstein, the leading Rabbi in our city, Dr. Stacy Spencer, the pastor of the fastest growing African American Church in the city, and the county mayor. Stacy has been a part of our pastor's network since day one, but my encounter with Rabbi Micah Greenstein and Rick Recht was only recent. A year prior I had been invited to what I believe was the first concert at a neutral hall sponsored by the National Civil Rights Museum. It was Micah's suggestion that we have the event for a second year and that my church host it. Inviting such a diverse group to gather at our church met with both criticism and approval both from members of the community and from our own staff. Although our critics had their reasons, the impact on those who attended, and on me especially, was profound.

What started as an awareness benefit designed to tear down the walls of racism and prejudice became the beginning of a deep friendship for me with Micah and Stacy. In fact, I've discovered that Stacy is a better preacher than I'll ever be and Micah knows more about the Christian faith than most Christians do. He is also one of the most gracious and humble men I know. One of the proudest moments of my life was when I opened the invitation to Micah's son's bar mitzvah. I wouldn't have missed it for the world. We all walked away from the "Tearing Down the Walls" event with the profound understanding that our relationship, our friendship, is being watched by all of our faith communities with cautious curiosity. How is it that in a city that is known for its problems with racism and prejudice there can be honest members of various faith communities making an effort to get to know each other on a *personal* level? Do you have any friends of another faith or color? Have you ever shared a meal with them? Have you ever had them to your home for dinner or been invited to theirs?

As I said at the beginning of this chapter, this is not a book about joining something. God knows there are enough organizations, enough churches, and enough synagogues to join. What puzzles me is how we all came to the conclusion that if you aren't a member of *my* organization you couldn't *possibly* be right. And unless you believe what I believe and worship as I worship we can't be friends. We can't work on missions' projects together or have dinner together, or invite each other to live life together. We have isolated and segregated and migrated so far away from those with whom we don't agree that it becomes impossible to love your neighbors. You can't find your neighbor, and if you do find him he looks just like you!

I confessed to Micah one day that he was only the second Jewish person I had really ever known. I met a young man in college who was Jewish and we became friends. But our friendship couldn't flourish because I was so dedicated to defending my tight little circle of beliefs. I thought that's what I was *supposed* to do. There wasn't room for a Jew in that circle. My friends were all people who shared my faith convictions. If I couldn't convert him, I didn't want to get too close to him. I was too insecure about the tiny little circle of conviction I had drawn around myself to let anyone who was different come in.

Micah sometimes signs his correspondence to me, "From your *second* Jewish friend." It's his kind, gentle, gracious way of affirming my meager effort. My story is not an unusual description of most of us. Most of us live very isolated lives, and we miss all the richness that God lavishes on those who find ways to flesh out the commandment of Jesus when he says, "Love one another."

My aim is not to get you to agree with one another. I think it will take God to make that happen. What I want is for us to love one another. Find practical ways to love one another. Take care of one another. Help one another. Befriend one another. Be kind to one another. Be gracious to one another. Reach out to one another. Be there for one another. In how many different ways can it be said? And yet something inside us all subtly moves us to label each other, and criticize each other, and cubbyhole each other, and run from each other, and fear each other, and hate each other, and go to war with each other, and on and on. It's a vicious game that we don't even intend to be playing.

There is just something that seems so reassuring, so comforting, so reaffirming, about knowing you are right and everyone else is wrong. You sleep better at night knowing that all is right with the world because you believe you are right with the world. But it can't be so! If you are right about everything then most of the rest of the world has to be wrong about everything. And that is a very small circle in which to live. But admittedly it takes courage, and a brave heart, and a strong constitution to move outside your comfort zone into the world of the unknown, into the world of the unexplained. It's uncomfortable for me to admit that when I invite Micah and his family to dinner at our home, I don't know if I need to prepare food a certain way. It's uncomfortable for me to ask him. It's uncomfortable to go to my Hispanic friend's home the very first time for his daughter's birthday party knowing I'm one of the only people who speaks English. But I have never come away from one of those experiences feeling embarrassed or ashamed. Those friends have done everything in their power to ease me into what they know is new territory for me. And it's only a small part of the thrill that awaits those who will take the plunge into new, cold waters of life.

I haven't changed my beliefs at all. But I have come to the conclusion that as sincerely as I believe what I believe, it is possible that I am sincerely wrong. Now I'd like to think not. I even hope not. But what kind of arrogance must a person have to believe that his or her narrow world view is right and the rest of humanity is wrong? How presumptuous is that? I was always taught that if you accept those into "fellowship," whatever that means, who don't share your doctrine, your theology, your beliefs, you're starting down a slippery slope. I have many colleagues that believe this with all their hearts, colleagues from many faith traditions.

And so we have divided ourselves by what we *can't* agree on rather than to unite behind what we *can* agree on. I can just hear the criticism now: "He's become a universalist, a heretic, a lunatic…" But I'd much rather stand before whatever God you believe in and confess that I loved too much, I accepted too many, than to run the risk of having to admit to God that I didn't love enough. That I didn't accept enough. It's relatively easy for me to believe what I believe. I'll bet it is for you too. But it's much more difficult to act on that belief, to live by that belief, to risk for that belief, and to sacrifice for that belief.

I met an African American pastor a few years ago.

41

A national consultant called me and asked me to meet with this pastor who had just moved from Chicago to Memphis, and who might not fully understand "Southern church politics." We met, and I did a pretty lousy job of convincing him I had much knowledge about the subject. His theology was and still is probably on the other end of the theological spectrum from my own. We didn't talk for several years after our first meeting. Last year he faced a sad disagreement with a small faction within his congregation that led to a very controversial ruling by a secular judge against him and several leaders in his congregation. He called for a vote of mass support from the Church community. On a whim, not believing my presence made any difference one way or another, I drove downtown to his church merely to show my support on the off chance that my being there might mean something to him. I assumed there would be hundreds of pastors from most of the large African American churches and maybe even some of the primarily white churches. I was stunned to find that only a handful of people, maybe forty, were at the luncheon. I think I was the only white person there. I know I was the only white pastor there. I followed him to the courthouse with members of his congregations and met the media where again, sadly, I was the only white person in sight. He came straight to my church after his court hearing. Although I couldn't meet him right that minute, I called him at home that night.

Frank said, "Can we be friends?"

I said, "Yes."

He said, "No, I mean apart from our churches."

"Yes," I said.

"No, I mean whether we agree on theology or not."

"Yes," I said.

It's as if we are so bound by our disagreements, we just can't believe a relationship could survive our differences of opinion and our convictions. Frank has become one of my best friends. He's prophetic. He regularly tells me where I'm wrong. He's expanded my world view on more than one occasion. Because of our friendship, we've moved way past theological disagreement. He called one week, in a bind. He had mistakenly made a commitment to speak in another church when he was scheduled to preach in his own church. He asked me to preach for him. I've heard Frank preach. He teaches preaching to seminary students. I felt as though I were standing in the shadow of one great preacher that night. I was the only white man in an African American congregation. The only place I have felt as loved and affirmed as I did with those dear people is with my friends at Hope. They treated me like family. What a rich experience!

People feel so much more comfortable when they can fit everyone into a little box that defines who they are. It's much easier to disagree, to avoid someone who doesn't fit in your box. But when we stop trying to define one another by the color of our skin, or the way we worship, or the club we belong to, or the political party we support, or the doctrine we defend so strenuously, it's so much easier to "Love our neighbors as ourselves." I read that somewhere. You may choose to agree or disagree with me. But wouldn't the world be a much better place if we'd quit finding reasons to distrust and/or hate each other and look for ways to trust and/or love each other? Wouldn't we be richer for it?

Okay, Let's Review:

1. Who have you befriended that believes differently from you?

2. Are your convictions getting in the way of your faith?

3. Who could you reach out to *today* that is different from you?

4. Instead of trying to *change* them, try to *understand* them.

5. Have you ever donated money for a worthy cause that may not be your cup of tea but you're pretty sure will impact the world in some way?

6. Do you know anyone of a different religion, race, or denomination that you could invite to lunch just to ask about what is important in their lives?

Just do it.

old traditions are fading
people are ready for a new thing

When I was a small boy, my parents used to take my sister and me to church every Sunday. The pastor's son was my best friend, so I was there just about every time the doors were opened. I'll go to my grave with the memory of sitting on the second row, making noise, doing anything to avoid listening. Although my friend's father was a nice guy, I can't remember one thing he said in all of those years. But to be fair, I can't remember one Sunday lunch my mother fixed either. I'm sure she must have prepared some excellent meals. She's a fabulous cook. But I can't recall one meal. However, I managed to eat every single Sunday. I suspect the pastor's messages and the Sunday School classes I attended had more of an influence on me than I can remember. They probably fed me more than I realized at the time. I'm sure I must have learned something at some level.

In junior high school my sister announced she wasn't going to church anymore, an idea that sounded good to me, and so we both revolted. And I can't remember going to church again for many years. Church always seemed irrelevant to me. The pastor, as sincere as he could be, often yelled at people (for effect, I suppose), referred to Greek and Hebrew words, and told stories that made no sense to a young boy struggling to find his identity as an adolescent. I never remember being inspired, or motivated, or comforted, or reassured. The only memory I have is being consistently bored out of my mind.

My experience wasn't different from many of the adults in that congregation and other churches around the city. Dads were thinking about their golf game, Moms were thinking about Sunday lunch. Kids were dreading the homework they had to do before returning to school Monday. Church was that way in the fifties, sixties, and seventies. Our pastor was pretty clear that *his* teachings, the teachings of *that* denomination, were the only really *true* teachings. I remember wondering why others didn't naturally see the necessity of joining our church. Even though I was pretty bored with it, I still couldn't imagine why there were so many religions. I couldn't fathom why most of the people didn't believe what I was taught to believe. I'm probably not telling you anything you didn't experience at the time.

You don't have to be a historian or a theologian to have heard about the decline of mainline denominations in the last thirty years. You don't have to follow television preachers to know that their target is limited to a rather narrow audience. Why? Old sectarian denominational fortresses are crumbling and being swept from the world scene. People are tired of being divided by religious beliefs, racism, and sectarianism. The words of Rodney King speak for many of us: "Why can't we just all get along?"

I believe the world is ready for a new thing. I believe people are ready for a new definition.

I mentioned my pastor friend from Chicago, Frank, who became my dear friend because I was willing to reach out and he reached back. We have breakfast, take our wives out for yogurt some Sunday nights; Lee and I love to go to the church Frank pastors. In short, he's my friend. Last year I was at a denominational meeting in Chicago with people who more or less "think and believe like I do." When I left Memphis that morning, I remembered Frank. He's from Chicago. We sometimes have a voice-mail relationship even though we're good friends.

I called and left him a message: "Hey Frank, I couldn't help but think of you. I'm headed to Chicago today. I know Chicago is your stomping ground so I wanted to give you a call to let you know I was thinking about you. I love you, man."

Frank left a message on my cell phone: "Funny you should call, Craig; actually I'm *in* Chicago, preaching at a church on the South Side."

I call back: "Frank, I can't believe it! Where? I'm in North Chicago, but if I get a chance, I might come hear you preach…"

Frank: "No man, you'll never make it. I'm on the South Side of Chicago. It would take you an hour and a half in traffic to get where I am. We'll hook up another time."

Me: "What is the exact address, Frank, just in case?"

And he left the address.

I was in meetings all day, at points frustrating meetings. Although some of my colleagues are close friends, others are not so much. We frustrate each other. I refuse to believe *exactly* what they believe and they refuse to believe *exactly* what I believe, *even though we're in the same denomination!* I'm not proud of that but it's true. It's a problem we're working on together. It's probably the main reason we meet. Recently we've started bring our wives to this annual meeting. It has improved the atmosphere significantly. Our wives won't allow us to sit around and pontificate all of the time. By their very presence they force us to interact on a more personal level and so it's good when they come.

However, at this particular meeting sans wives, I had seen one of my close friends pour his heart out to the group that very morning, but nobody was listening…really. I had to catch him at the break and plead with him not to fly home. He was feeling pretty ignored, pretty unappreciated. His wife had cancer. Of all times, he needed a group of friends now. But he couldn't find it in that crowd, nor could I. I went down to the opulent restaurant for dinner, in fact, the last person to be seated at the table. The waiter was standing ready to take my order. I looked around the table and said to myself, "I can't do it." And then to the others, "You all will have to excuse me. I have an appointment in South Chicago and I can't miss it." I jumped in the car and drove to South Chicago with my hair on fire and walked into the church just as my friend Frank was about to preach. I was the only white guy there. He smiled and said to the people, "I'd like to introduce to you my good friend Craig Strickland. He came all the way from Memphis to hear me preach." And afterwards I was invited to the pastor's study for dinner with Frank and the key leaders of their church—a group of people I had only met that night. And they treated me far, far more like family than did my own colleagues. I felt at home. Sometimes I feel as welcomed—like family—in an African American church, or a Hispanic church, or a church in Mexico or Ecuador as I do in my own.

I believe people are longing to see a new thing. People are hungry for a leadership that is more committed to unconditional love than to doctrinal purity—more committed to loving thy neighbor than to being theologically correct. People are aching to see their pastor admit publicly that he doesn't have all of life's answers and that there is enormous benefit in working along side others in the faith community. People are just looking for open-minded, selfless, servant leadership; and if they could just find that kind of leadership in their places of worship, the business of conquering the problems of the world would be so much more rewarding and fulfilling.

Among the many things Jesus said, perhaps one of the most important was this: "A new command I give you: Love one another. As I have loved you, so you must love one another. By this all men will know that you are my disciples, if you love one another" (John 13:34–35). I wonder what would happen if all the Christians in the world followed these words of Jesus? I wonder if we could make a real difference in the world?

Why is it that we have such a hard time with the idea of loving people who are different? Love seems to be much easier to accomplish with those who are like us. But for those who look different, or act different, or believe differently, we seem to have a much tougher time. And yet the Scripture says in 1 John 2:9–11,

> Anyone who claims to be in the light but hates his
> brother is still in the darkness. Whoever loves his
> brother lives in the light, and there is nothing in him
> to make him stumble. But whoever hates his brother
> is in the darkness and walks around in the darkness;
> he does not know where he is going, because the
> darkness has blinded him.
>
> 1 John 2:9–11

Is that you? Are you saying, "Yeah, that's right? Why can't we just all get along?" Maybe it's time for you to talk to your pastor. Now, I'll have to warn you as a part of the clergy community, that a lot of us clergy will be really, really threatened by your admonition. In fact, I expect to be criticized roundly for sharing my little secret: The world is changing. Leaders need to change, too. Leaders need to lead. People are hungry for leaders who have a Kingdom mindset. People are starving for a leader who is willing to serve others instead of expecting to be served. Is that the other part of the secret? As far as I know, nowhere does the Scripture indicate that heaven will be divided into little rooms to separate those whose beliefs differ. Now I wouldn't presume to be so arrogant as to tell you that people like me, people who believe what I believe, will be the only ones there. Others may make those assumptions, not me. I know what the Bible says and I haven't sold out. I still hold tightly to my convictions. But I'm also willing to acknowledge that, as sincerely as I believe what I believe, I could be sincerely wrong. And that gives me all kinds of freedom. It gives me the freedom to reach out with open arms to all kinds of people that would never end up in my tight little circle of convictions.

Okay, Let's Review:

1. Have you ever worshipped in a church of another denomination or race?

2. Have you ever attended a service in a synagogue?

3. Have you considered that they believe they are as right in their beliefs as you are in yours?

4. Have you ever been criticized for your faith? Why or why not? Was the criticism justified?

5. Are you ready for a "new thing"? What would that look like for you? What have you done to make it happen?

Just do it.

does my life really count?

If God were to produce one of those TV shows that are now cultural phenomena many of us watch every week, how would He change you?

Makeover shows are the rage right now and there are many different types of them out there for all types of audiences. You can make over your house, your car, your body, your self-esteem, or your musical ability. If you can think of something to makeover, there is a better than average chance that someone has created a television show about it.

I'm going to confess something to you today. It's another part of my dark side that I'd rather you not tell anyone. I don't want anyone but you to know it. I don't want people talking all over town. There's one makeover show in particular that I think is curiously interesting. It's called *What Not to Wear*. Now I'll admit, I'm so addicted, we Tivo the thing and watch it every night. The premise is that these two style specialists find a frumpy, out of date, whacked out, often stubborn, woman or sometimes a man and talk her or him into being made completely over. The soon-to-be-made-overs have to go to New York, with all their tired, worn-out clothes, get criticized on national television, take $5,000 for a new wardrobe, shop till they drop, and, with the help of style experts, they go home a new person. Now I don't think I've missed an episode (I already confessed it's an addiction), but I've never seen a person that didn't go home feeling like a brand new person. Now if I were talking about my addiction to college basketball, all you guys would be nodding your heads in agreement. But can you see what an embarrassing confession mine is? There are no guys nodding their heads—not that there aren't some of you that would do well to get in touch with your feminine side—but the fact remains that these people go home feeling like they are brand new people!

What would *you* think if you could be made into anything or anyone else? What would that look like for you?

When I watch the show, there's something admirable about some of the contestants. They're willing to get on national television in front of you and me and the entire free world, and go after their dreams. Most of these people are taking a huge risk to follow a dream. At the same time, when I look at some of these contestants, before and after, I wonder if I'm looking at the same person. And yet, at the end they always seem to have so much more confidence. They seem so much more self-assured. I can't help but wonder if any one of them has ever asked the question, "God, is this who you made me to be?"

We are all being made into someone every moment of every day. And I think the question is, are we being made into all that we are meant to be or are we settling for something false? Are we settling for a distorted version of who we could be or are we becoming a new creation? The Apostle Paul once said, "Therefore, if anyone is in Christ, he is a new creation; the old has gone, the new has come" (2 Corinthians 5:17)!

God leaves the door open to change us, to shape us and to form us into all that we are meant to be. And in my opinion, the journey of being made into all we are meant to be is a journey of finding one's true self. Finding out who we truly are is probably the most important challenge of our lives.

What I've discovered from my own life and what I've learned from others in almost forty years of living the Christian life is that in the place of my true self, I often create many false images of myself along the way. I am reminded again and again of the irony that doesn't escape me for one second: that I am always faced with a very real temptation to be someone that I'm not—to be whoever I may think you want or expect me to be. As I seek to engage with you, in a message of finding and becoming our true selves, I'm always tempted to fake it. And I think that is a temptation that we all face more often than we'd like to think.

If there is really a special person that God has created us to be, then I think there are also many false images that you and I have created along the way. To become our true self, we first have to come to terms with, to face, our false self. Some authors define the false self as *what I have, what I can do, or what others think of me.*

Let me suggest a few visual examples that display a bit of the disparity that often exists between the outer layer we present to the world and our inner core, which is who we really are and which hides inside of our impenetrable outer layer. And how do these visual examples help us to learn how to treat each other so we can unravel what's really precious and true and beautiful on the inside of each of us?

For a moment will you visualize with me pieces of fruit representing various types of human personalities? There is the *Tender-hearted Kiwi* personality. The outer layer of the kiwi is fuzzy and brown. What's that about? It stands as a stark contrast to what is going on inside at the inner core of the kiwi. Inside it's a different color, it's a different texture. Its outer layer and inner core are vastly different.

To get at what is really precious and beautiful inside of a kiwi personality, we have to treat the person tenderly, with a lot of care. If we're too harsh or too strong with them inside a kiwi personality, we can just crush them. We squeeze the very life out of them. We destroy what is precious and true and beautiful about that person.

On the other end of the spectrum, there is the *Hard-hearted Coconut* personality. The outer layer of the coconut is hard and hairy. It's scratchy if you rub it against your cheek. It's like an impenetrable shield. And we know people like this, right? People who have a hard outer layer that's protecting and hiding what's really happening on the inside. But the inside of the coconut is entirely different. Though it may be a little bit flaky, it's delightful. To get at what's precious and beautiful inside the coconut personality, we have to treat this person with love, but we may have to be a little more direct. We may have to ask questions that are a bit more pointed. We may have to speak a little more truth to the coconut.

Some of us are like the *Banana*. It has an eye pleasing outer layer. When you peel it back you find a soft, tender inner core that is easily bruised by harsh, insensitive words. If you don't take the time to get to know the banana-type personality, you bruise this person without even knowing it.

Now in the midst of all this variety, we have the *Apple*. The apple, I think, is the ideal personality. You and I would probably like to think the apple is more representative of us, because the outer layer of the apple isn't all that different from its inner core. The outer layer of the apple is pretty consistent with the inside. There's not a whole lot of difference. Outside it's not too hard, unlike the coconut; it's not too tender, like the kiwi. It's just right and appropriately in a way contains and protects what's true inside. I think most of us would prefer to think we are like the apple.

But in reality, I think we are much more like the *Melon*. The outer layer of a watermelon is quite peculiar. It comes in many sizes, shapes, colors, and textures. The outside is relatively thick and a little hard but not quite like the coconut. However, the inside is pink or red or orange or sometimes a fascinating lime green. Sometimes it has seeds, sometimes not. But at its prime, at the peak of its ripeness, the inner core is very soft, almost mushy, and always sweet. Its outer layer is exceptionally different from its inner core.

And with persons like this, if you're not careful, if you don't treat them with special care and handle them with wisdom and concern, you'll end up with quite a mess on your hands. Try dropping a watermelon and you'll catch a glimpse of what I mean.

Although most of us would like to think we're the apple, with an outer layer that is consistent with our inner core, in reality, most of us are much more like the melon, with an outer layer that is vastly different from what is truly going on inside.

Many of us learn very early in our lives to present ourselves to the world in certain ways to gain acceptance, attention, or maybe approval. For most of us it starts with our parents. And then we crave the attention and approval of our peers. And we'll invent any kind of false image to gain that acceptance. No one makes it through middle school or high school without deeply desiring to be accepted and willing to do almost anything to get it.

How about you? How about the story of your life? What have you done to earn the praise of others? On the other hand, what has earned you the ridicule or scorn of others? And how much do you rely on it today? If you lay those two questions side by side, you have your false self: the person that you are trying to be just to get a little love and to avoid rejection. In essence, the false self is how we have learned to survive in this world. Because people instinctively accept or reject, approve or condemn, one another conditionally. We act a certain way, or achieve certain things, or perform at a certain standard to gain the acceptance and approval of others. We feel it's the only way we can get it.

The curious dichotomy is that God created us to be loved unconditionally. That is our origin; that is how we were created. If you have never experienced unconditional love, if you have never been loved just because you are "you," with no strings attached, then you have very quickly learned how to adapt. You learn how to be noticed, to be recognized, to be praised, to be accepted, to be beautiful, to be loved. In short, through adapting to earn love and avoid pain, we learned to pretend. And the unfortunate reality is that what begins as a role becomes an identity, and you and I are transformed into someone and something that is not authentic. We are shaped into someone that is far less than what we are meant to be. You can never become the person you were *created* to be until you are willing to embrace the person that you *currently are*.

As long as we pretend, we choose the false self. So the question becomes: How can I come out of hiding and step toward the life that God created for me? What steps do I need to take for my extreme makeover?

The first step is to start being honest with yourself. Every single person who's ever walked the face of the earth, except for Jesus Christ himself, has created a false image of his or her real self. We can't escape it. There's no need to feel guilty about it or ashamed of it. It's part of the human condition. It's part of the human journey. The longer we live trying to be who we are not, the longer we live outside God's design for our lives, It will sooner or later begin to take its toll. We find ourselves exhausted after trying so hard to be who we are not. And our bodies pay the price. That brings us to the point of realizing who we truly are without God: broken people in need of an extreme makeover. However, our tendency is to avoid or deny the truth. To push it down. To suppress it.

The first step to become who we are truly meant to be is to embrace the false self we've created along the way. It requires finding safe people with whom we can be honest, people who will encourage and welcome us as fallible human beings that God loves unconditionally. We need people in our lives who will accept us that way.

Do you have any safe people in your life? Do you have anyone in your life with whom you can be completely honest and who will be completely honest with you? If you can share those deepest, darkest parts of who you are—and we all have them—with a person who will look you in the eye and still accept you just as you are, that's safe. Do you have any safe friends in your life? I am fortunate to be able to turn in a variety of directions to find safe people to share my life with. Lee has been the most reliable and long-term safe haven for me. Recently, when I felt like I needed the one person who knew me best, both my strengths and my weaknesses, to give me an honest evaluation, it was Lee to whom I turned. She has always been there to accept me as unconditionally as any one human being can. However, that's a lot of pressure for a soul-mate. So I have cultivated three other relationships over the years that are safe for me and from whom I always seek counsel when I have potentially life-changing decisions to make. If all of them are leaning together in a certain direction, like it or not, I listen. They represent completely different worlds to me. All three live or have lived their lives in different professions than mine. If I can't take their counsel, I feel that I'm simply not willing to allow God to speak to me.

Frank Norfleet is one of those men. He has been like a father to me for over twenty-five years. I love my mother and father very much and I would do anything in the world for them. They would do the same for me. However, twenty-five years ago, as a young pastor, I looked to Frank, a very successful Christian businessman to give me sound, practical, wise, godly advice. Frank is a remarkable man in his own right—after serving under General Patton as a young soldier in World War II, he went on to grow and eventually sell a family business to an international firm. What I have always loved about Frank is that he has taken me under his wing like a son. Frank has taught me much of what I know about leadership. He believed in me long before just about anybody else did. He believed in me long before I had accomplished anything. And he twice kept me from leaving the ministry with his frank, loving, upfront, wise style of leadership. In his 80s today, he and I regularly meet for lunch. He has helped me grow a church, raise a family, and navigate almost all of the stormy waves of life. As long as I live, I will never be able to repay him for his many kindnesses to me and my family. In the last years, he has adopted my boys as well. He now offers them much of the same wisdom, encouragement, and support he has offered me all these years. Now he has been a mentor for two generations in my family while he has provided the same loving guidance and direction for his children and grandchildren as well.

I have also been in an accountability group with the president of a Christian college and a Christian psychologist for almost fifteen years. We meet every other week and talk about our personal lives, our business challenges, as well as our hopes and dreams for the future. These guys fly just below the radar screen. Although I pastor a large church and reside in the city I grew up in, very few people know the impact these two men have had on my life. In fact, not many people know who they are. Although they teach from time to time at Hope, rarely does anyone recognize them as two of the most important people in my life.

So there are at least four people (and a number of other very close friends) who know almost every detail of my life. If I were about to make a major decision, I would ask for counsel from each of them. I have never moved in a direction contrary to their counsel.

In addition to having safe people in my life, I need to accept my true identity. I've got to replace the false lies on which my identity is based—what I have, what I do, what others think of me, and find my true identity in the God who created me. An identity grounded in God means that I am able to see myself as someone who is deeply loved by God. When you think of who you are, is that the first thing that comes to your mind?

God loves us deeply in the midst of our brokenness and weakness. Our identity is not based on anything we have done or anything we have become apart from God. God tells us not to be afraid. He affirms His love for us: "Do not be afraid for I have redeemed you. I have called you by your name. You are mine. You are precious in my eyes because you are honored and I love you" (Isaiah 43:1 & 4 NLT). He assures us that He will never leave us. "The mountains may depart, the hills are shaken, but my love for you will never leave you. And my covenant of peace for you will never be shaken" (Isaiah 54:10).

So we need to renew our minds with the truth that God loves us and accepts us just for who we are. We are loved and cherished. God fully comprehends the depth of our darkness. It just means He offers us a way to come to Him. But we find our true selves safely cradled in the arms of a loving Heavenly Father. Will you choose to embrace this love? In a world that is longing for authenticity and yet settles for less, will you choose to embrace the freeing love of God? In his book, *The Wisdom of Tenderness,* Brennan Manning says:

> When the primacy of love is subordinated to doctrinal correctness and orthodox exegesis, cool cordiality and polite indifference masquerade as love among theologians, biblical scholars, and faculties across the land. When absolute control and rigid obedience pose as love within the family and the local faith-community, we produce trained cowards rather than Christian persons.[1]

I could not agree more. Are you known for assisting God in the process of creating true Christian people, or are you producing trained cowards?

There are far too many melons in this world. Will you choose to be an apple? Will you choose to be free? Will you choose to be loved? Will you choose to be made, or rather re-made, into the person God intends you to be? Finding out who we truly are, on the inside, is the key to true peace. All of our happiness depends on it.

Okay, Let's Review:

1. If you could be made over into a different person, who would you look like?

2. If you were a fruit, what fruit would best describe you?

3. What is one thing you can change about yourself *today?*

4. Who is the person in your life who comes the closest to loving you unconditionally?

5. In your life, who has failed at love so badly that their action calls for forgiveness?

6. Have you taken any steps toward forgiveness?

7. Who would you say are *your* mentors?

8. In what areas of your life do you seek the counsel of a mentor?

9. Are there areas of your life that are closed to input from others? Name them.

10. Who have you picked out to mentor through life?

Just do it.

you don't shoot your wounded

The military would find the very statement quite ludicrous. In fact, all branches of the military have a no-one-gets-left-behind policy. They will go to any extreme to recover their soldiers. And no branch of our military would ever consider shooting someone who is wounded. On the contrary, everything possible would be done to assure his or her rescue and healing. At the very least, that level of care is expected, even demanded, by those who protect our freedom.

So, why is it that the only army in the world that shoots its own wounded is the Christian army? Almost every faith community is guilty:

- Divorce has become the unpardonable sin. When a couple files for divorce, the church quietly turns its back. One or both parties quietly slip away from the church until the mess from their sins is completed, then one or both return.

- Alcoholism and/or drug addiction are seen as sins

that happen outside the church. When one gets sober or successfully completes drug treatment, he or she is *then* welcomed back into the fold. And yet the drug of choice for many fine church-going folk is prescription medication. And no one seems to notice or care.

- Addiction to pornography is arguably the fastest growing addiction in America and yet rarely is it mentioned in the church. Efforts to help those who are willing to admit their struggles are few and far between.

- HIV/AIDS is the leprosy of our generation. We only talk about it as sin and almost never seek to aid those whose lives are being slowly eaten away by this terminal disease. And yet the largest group of those contracting HIV/Aids in our country this year is women. We simply sweep the problem under the rug if we sweep at all.

I could list many more. Is there any hope that religion can help us come together to solve our problems? Or is religion the problem? My point is that we are starting to define ourselves by the things we're against rather than what we are for. As I said earlier, that circle becomes smaller and smaller.

There are people who walk into our church and make the sign of the cross, a good indication that they have a Roman Catholic background. Many of them are members of our church. Some of them like to say they are Presbyterians in Memphis but when they go home they are Catholic. I've never tried to stop them from making the sign of the cross. I wouldn't dream of it. Why should it matter to me if this act helps them feel closer to God? Isn't that the ultimate goal?

I have a friend in a small town in Mexico who watches a man walk by his church every day and make the sign of the cross. This man has a reputation in this small town. He's had several affairs and is sleeping around right now. But every day he walks by my friend's Protestant church and makes the sign of the cross. And yet he never darkens the door. My friend asks, "Why? Why won't he come in? He obviously knows we're here, he comes by and makes the sign of the cross every day."

A couple of years ago during a worship service an associate pastor in our church turned to me and said, "I don't know if you know it, but we've got some strippers that come to Hope.

I said, "How do you know that?" I'll admit it. I couldn't help but wonder if he had been visiting a few of the clubs in town.

But he said, "I've been counseling a couple." Truthfully, I knew of a couple myself. God only knows how many I don't know who come. But you want to know why they strip? A woman can make *five times* more money stripping than just about anything else she can do. Some of these women come to church every week for months. Stripping during the week and coming to church on Sundays! Can you imagine how they must feel when they walk through that door for the first time? What kind of culture does a church have to create that would allow a stripper to come to church for months while she is still stripping simply to give her the opportunity to experience God's love instead of the church's judgment and condemnation?

I read somewhere that Jesus had a special affinity for just these kinds of people. The story goes like this,

> The religious scholars and Pharisees led in a woman who had been caught in an act of adultery. They stood her in plain sight of everyone and said, "Teacher, this woman was caught red-handed in the act of adultery. Moses, in the Law, gives orders to stone such persons. What do you say?" They were trying to trap him into saying something incriminating so they could bring charges against him.
>
> Jesus bent down and wrote with his finger in the dirt. They kept at him, badgering him. He straightened up and said, "The sinless one among you, go first: Throw the stone." Bending down again, he wrote some more in the dirt.
>
> Hearing that, they walked away, one after another, beginning with the oldest. The woman was left alone. Jesus stood up and spoke to her. "Woman, where are they? Does no one condemn you?"
>
> "No one, Master."
>
> "Neither do I," said Jesus. "Go on your way. From now on, don't sin."
>
> John 8:1–12 The Message

Think back to my friend from Mexico who wondered why the adulterous man wouldn't come into his church. I asked him, "Would you rather have the man embroiled in his fifth affair walk *by* your church or walk *into* your church?" It's all in the culture the Church creates.

Years ago Eli Morris began teaching me the art of servant-leadership, or how to love others by serving them unconditionally. You see, Eli had befriended a young African American woman when she was still in public high school. She eventually had her first out-of-wedlock child and dropped out of school. But Eli would not allow her to drop out of his sphere of influence. Eli continued to reach out to her over the years, calling every few weeks, helping with a utility bill here and there, buying groceries occasionally, and showing up at just the right time with an outstretched hand of unconditional love. I knew *of* her, but I didn't really *know* her.

Several years after Eli joined the staff at Hope to help me with this burgeoning ministry, he got a call from this young woman. Unfortunately, he was out of town, so I took the call. She was in a panic, and needed food to feed her babies (now there were four little mouths to feed). In Eli's absence I could think of nothing else to do but to respond to her plea for help. With skepticism, I went to the supermarket and bought about a hundred dollars of staples: milk, bread, potatoes, peanut butter, and hamburger meat…anything that I thought she could feed the kids but with no room for extravagance. I called to get her address and delivered the food to her home.

When I arrived, I insisted on taking the food to the kitchen of the poor, small, dingy, apartment. I wanted to open the refrigerator for myself to see just how much she really needed the food. I was stunned to discover nothing in the freezer but a small, half-filled pot of watery soup. In the refrigerator I found a half used bottle of ketchup and the remnants of a jar of mustard. And that was it. Nothing more. Nada. So I gathered her young family in a circle in the tiny living room and held hands and prayed for them. I wasn't even quite sure how to pray, and until this day I don't remember what I said. But to tell you the truth, I don't think what I said was all that important. I don't think she remembered what I said. I think she remembered what I did—unconditional love. I saw it first in Eli's life. He wasn't expecting this young woman to *become* anything necessarily. His help wasn't conditioned by her growth in any way. He was just reaching out with the unconditional love of God.

What if the faith community decided to define itself by its desire to help the ill, the troubled, the addicted, and the poor? To open its doors to those who may not yet believe or if they do believe are not quite ready to live like it? What if we chose to define ourselves not by a set of doctrines but by our willingness to open loving arms? What if we were to agree to disagree about nonessentials and find the lowest common denominator that we *could* agree on and joined together at *that* point to change our world? What if we quit shooting our wounded and started to bandage them? What if we stopped criticizing what we *don't* like about one another or what we can't agree about and started tearing down walls? What if we joined hands and worked together instead of locking arms to keep others out? What if it all started with you? What if you didn't wait for a clergy leader or a business leader or a political leader and just started making changes yourself?

Almost five years ago I met my Latino friend Greg quite by chance. He was a fairly new pastor in town who had started a Latino church the hard way. While his wife worked, Greg strolled the children through his neighborhood inviting his friends to come to his church. After a grueling two years, his group had grown to a hundred people or so. In an effort to increase the size of his congregation, he had decided to bring a well known Latino singer/songwriter to town for a concert for the city's Hispanic community. Anticipating a huge crowd, he went from church to church looking for a large church that would rent him their facility. With little but a vision from God, he was hoping somebody would come forward and reach out to his people with an outstretched hand of love. After being told "No" by more than twenty churches, Greg came to Hope.

Bob Russell, who works in my office, responded to Greg's request by saying, "Let me talk to our senior pastor about it and get back to you." Greg was certain he would be told "No" one more time, but Bob and I saw it as a great opportunity to work together with a pastor who was reaching people we could never reach.

So I said, "Tell this young man we don't *rent* our facilities. However we will *loan* their church the facilities under one condition: they let our people come and serve. We want Greg's church to let our people greet at the doors, clean up afterwards, and provide for any needs they might have."

Greg said, "I speak pretty good English, but I'm not sure I understand what you're saying. Are you saying that you won't take our money and the only way we can use your facility is if we allow your people to serve us?"

Bob said, "Yes, that's right."

As you can imagine, churches aren't very good at serving one another and so Greg was taken aback so much he asked to meet me.

I agreed to meet with Greg, but only if we could meet at his church. See, it's quite common for pastors of large churches to invite pastors of small churches into their spacious, well appointed offices for a meeting. But for a pastor of a large church to go to the small church of a Latino pastor didn't happen very often. I thought it would be a good way to serve Greg. Jesus used a similar approach, but he washed feet. Now I wasn't really ready to wash Greg's feet. I was ready to settle for loaning our church. Not as dramatic but for sure, Greg needed the church more!

He asked me to come to lunch first, at a small restaurant across the street from his church where I discovered they had closed the restaurant just for Bob and me. We must have eaten for two hours. They wouldn't let us stop! It was then that I realized that while I thought I was going to be serving my new friend, he showed me far more about service than I knew. I have worked very closely with him on a variety of projects for almost five years and I've come to learn that as a people, Latinos understand servant leadership better than most Anglos ever will. I learned that serving others was much bigger than any plan I could have ever thought of. I realized the ramifications could be long reaching.

My wife read a book about the environment recently. We have never paid much attention to the fact that how we live has an impact on the environment (another one of my sins). Our daughter, Emily, has encouraged us to recycle for years. In fact, in my experience, the next generation is far more concerned about our impact on the environment than my generation. It's as if the older generation is less knowledgeable and less willing to believe that they really could make a difference. So Lee very quietly started recycling. She didn't really say anything to anyone. She just started doing it. She didn't wait on me to provide the leadership. She just started doing it. She started collecting empty bottles and cans and paper. She started looking for ways to recycle old clothes. She didn't ask anybody. She didn't say anything. She just did it. Now do you think Lee can change the world with her meager efforts? I doubt it. But she's changing *her* world. And guess what? I have taken notice. I'm feeling a little guilty that I haven't been such a good steward of the world's resources. In fact, I'm starting to feel a *lot* guilty. And I'm finding myself using Lee's storage boxes and bags to recycle the bottles and cans I use up. See? One person, doing his or her small part, inspires another to do his or her small part, and eventually, we change the world. It's not a pyramid scheme. It's not a ponzi scheme. It's simply people humbly doing their part. If we could just stop attacking and start attending to the needs of others, we would quietly begin to change the world. Let's put our guns away.

Okay, Let's Review:

1. Is there a person in your life you've unwittingly "shot at" that probably needs your support now more than ever?

2. Your actions most likely didn't reflect your heart. What can you do to make amends?

3. What impact is your lifestyle having on the environment?

4. What is one thing you can do today that will change that behavior?

Just do it.

you can do more together than alone

I'm sure you've been hearing about it. Google "largest transfer of wealth" and you'll see how many people are talking about it. Many experts contend that we'll see the largest transfer of wealth in history in our generation. I know, I know, you're thinking, "Maybe so, but I'm sure not seeing any of it." That may be true, but we still live in the wealthiest nation on earth. In fact, according to an article by author Anup Shah:

- About half the world—nearly three billion people—live on less than two dollars a day.

- Nearly a billion people entered the 21st century unable to read a book or sign their names.

- Less than one percent of what the world *spends* every year on weapons would have put every child into a school by the year 2000, and yet it didn't happen.

- The wealthiest nation on Earth has the widest gap between rich and poor of any industrialized nation.

- 20% of the population in the developed nations consumes 86% of the world's goods.

- "The lives of 1.7 million children will be needlessly lost this year [2000] because world governments have failed to reduce poverty levels."

- "The combined wealth of the world's 200 richest people hit $1 trillion in 1999; the combined income of the 582 million people living in the 43 least developed countries is $146 billion."

- About ten percent, a tithe, of the world's 20 wealthiest people would pay the incomes of over five hundred million people in forty-three countries.

- "Approximately 790 million people in the developing world are still chronically undernourished, almost two-thirds of whom reside in Asia and the Pacific."

- According to UNICEF, 30,000 children die each day due to poverty. And they "die quietly in some of the poorest villages on earth, far removed from the scrutiny and the conscience of the world. Being meek and weak in life makes these dying multitudes even more invisible in death."

- Water problems affect half of humanity: Some 1.1 billion people in developing countries have inadequate access to water, and 2.6 billion lack basic sanitation.

- Some 1.8 million child deaths each year are as a result of diarrhea.[2]

Now these statistics are pretty overwhelming, aren't they? Nevertheless, we will still see the greatest transfer of wealth in our life time. What will we do about that? I've learned a valuable lesson over the years that I believe with all my heart. *You cannot out give God.* You may try, but it is utterly impossible. Now that's not to say that if you give away all your money, God will give you back even more. Maybe He will. But maybe He won't. It's not about your money. It's about your life. If you give away all your money, whether God gives you more back or not, you will live a richer life than you could ever have imagined.

Along with a group of friends I have met over the years, I have been trying as hard as I know how to out give God. Why? Because we have experienced the blessing that comes with this attempt over and over.

My son, Tucker, joined the Global Missions Department at Hope several years ago when he saw our church building a school in Quito, Ecuador. We were in the early stages of construction, digging footings by hand, when a group of older men invited Tucker to go with them at the last minute. Because he was uncertain of what he wanted to do with his life anyway, the timing could not have been more perfect. He saw young elementary-aged children packed into a few rooms of a rented building in one of the poorest areas of Quito, trying to get at least a few years of education. His heart was touched deeply by the needs of these young children and he returned home with a new vision for his life. He *made an appointment* to come see me! I said, "Tuck, you don't need an appointment, just come on over to the house." But he wouldn't hear of it. He came to his "appointment" with notebook in hand and said, "Dad, how do I raise $180,000? I am going to spend the next years of my life seeing that school in Ecuador get built and I'm going to raise the money." And he did.

He certainly didn't do it alone. And there were two incredibly talented professional chefs that made it all happen. But together they created a meals program for working moms at Hope. Busy moms could buy five or six meals for a hundred dollars or so, prepared under the direction of professional chefs, who added the pizzazz to the meals so we could call them gourmet. They used volunteers for the majority of the preparation. The meals, shrink wrapped, frozen, and ready to thaw and eat in twenty minutes, raised enough money to complete the school in eighteen months, almost two years ahead of time. When Tucker speaks of his experience building the school, he says, "My only disappointment is that I didn't partner with local churches. That partnership would have assured the long-term viability of the school and provided jobs and ministry opportunities for members of participating churches as well. I've learned my lesson. I'll always partner with other pastors to serve their churches." Tucker has just learned the value of servant leaders serving other servant leaders.

When I joined hands with a network of pastors in my own city, two things happened. I learned there are egocentric leaders in every church, in every neighborhood, in every city, and in every country, all over the world. Many of these leaders will never change. That's just a fact. But I've discovered other leaders all over the world who are determined to break the cultural stigma of egocentric leadership and are modeling servant-leadership wherever they go. I've also learned that when those leaders are connected through relationships of love and when those leaders set aside their differences, we *can* change our world!

I have also learned that the network of pastors who are now my friends in Memphis is the kind of network needed in cities all over the world. Most pastor networks are apostolic alliances. One pastor at the top of the heap is the leader of all. The Memphis network has no apostle. It is a group of equals.

I never realized that most pastors share two very dark little secrets. We are jealous, and we are territorial. We don't like getting too close to one another because we're afraid some will steal our members or steal some of our "trade secrets." Our church attempted to organize several conferences in Memphis to share with other pastors what we've learned about what makes a church grow, but we were disappointed to discover that, for whatever reason, people simply wouldn't come. It could well be that just about every large, growing Church in America was holding some type of conference, I don't know. But I do know that when my friend Greg asked me to teach the same material for Spanish-speaking pastors, the results were astounding. Not all pastors in the cities we have visited have wanted to serve each other. But we've seen pockets of receptivity, which have made the effort well worth the cost.

Last week I was in Reynosa, Mexico, with two dear friends who are pastors in the network of churches we began in Memphis almost five years ago. I would never have dreamed that a Latino pastor, a charismatic pastor, and a Presbyterian pastor could work hand in hand to encourage the pastors of the city of Reynosa to develop strategies that would change their city.

My Latino friend asked me to teach Church Growth Principles to Spanish-speaking people around the world and that's what we've been doing the last five years. I teach; he translates. Sometimes others translate. And now we have added several new elements to our teaching. We're starting to talk about spiritual darkness and poverty, and illness, and illiteracy in the developing countries in which we teach.

While in Reynosa meeting with pastors, I was taken to the ministry of a small, struggling church that is positioned right on the edge of the city's garbage dump. The church's ministry is pretty much targeted to the people who live in the dump and the prostitutes who work at the prostitution center a few blocks from the church. The church has little money, few people, and fewer resources to serve thousands of people that call the city dump home. The older children living in the dump get up every morning and search the dump for new things to eat or sell. I visited one of thousands of families that live there. I met a grandmother with no legs. The pastor of this small church found her right before the infection took her life and the church paid to have her legs amputated to save her life. So there she sat in her wheel chair, eating a bowl of God knows what, with flies flying around the bowl, while she looked after five children under the age of seven who were playing in the filth and squalor of the place they call home. There is a pig pen where they raise hogs about ten feet from their dinner table. The stench is almost unbearable. With no electricity, running water, heat, or air conditioning, they live in small shacks built by a well meaning church in Louisiana. The image is etched in my memory of this beautiful little four-year-old girl trying to change the diaper of an eighteen-month-old.

I have joined together with my friends from Hope, some servant-leader pastors in Reynosa and my missions-minded son to change the life of that little girl whose beautiful, sweet little face is still burned into my memory. I was talking to a new friend I met a few months ago about that little girl. My son Taylor was standing there and mentioned a small group of men he intended on taking to Reynosa to see this scene for themselves. My new friend, Russell, said to Taylor, "How many men are you taking and when do you want to go? I'm a pilot and I'd be glad to fly four or five men down there. I'd like to see it for myself." These men represent some of the wealth I wrote about earlier. I had no idea Russell had a plane. We were just talking. Taylor had been telling Russell how each night he had a group from Hope working there, he'd take their leftovers from dinner to the family he knew in the dump. He told Russell how he always liked to take a couple of people with him so they could see for themselves.

The collective wealth of that small group of men could fund projects for the foreseeable future: medical clinics for the ill; soup kitchens for the hungry; neighborhood grocery stores to provide fairly priced food for the poor, and churches for those who live their lives in spiritual darkness.

Servant-leadership is not a new concept. Even though human nature doesn't naturally move us to serve others, more and more authors, secular and Christian, are writing about the improvement in morale, motivation, and job performance when leaders serve those who work for them.

Bruce Carroll joined our staff at Hope about seven years ago. Almost every pastor of every church has a horror story to tell about his relationship with a director or minister of worship who simply refused to serve, insisting that the pastor didn't know anything about music and certainly wasn't qualified to offer his opinion, much less provide leadership in this crucial area of a church's life and ministry. I have my own fair share of war stories. But when I met Bruce, I met a new breed of leader. When he first joined the staff, in one of our initial encounters Bruce said, "Craig, you will never have to worry about me undermining your work here at Hope. I believe God called you to the work you do as He has called me, and my job is to serve you. You can trust me, you'll see. I'll always have your back."

You wouldn't necessarily know that Bruce has won numerous Grammy and Dove awards, the public's way of acknowledging greatness in the world of secular and Christian music. Bruce has recorded and produced multiple records and CDs over a lifetime of writing and singing Christian music. He is known all over the world for the mark he has left on the music world. In fact, it's not uncommon for someone to come up after one of our services and ask for Bruce to sign a CD that he has recorded. In my life as a leader, I've only one time been asked to sign anything for anyone. I was filled with excitement when one Saturday night after a service a man came to me to ask me to sign his bulletin. I was sure that finally someone knew who I was. However, it quickly dawned on me that he was a member of the recovery community. He had been charged with Driving Under the Influence and some judge was making the leader of various recovery groups sign a statement acknowledging that he had been attending groups. Although I was mildly crestfallen to find that I wasn't the object of his admiration but merely a "get out of jail free" card, I was elated to discover that finally, after many years of opening the doors of the church to the recovery community, we had at last been adopted as part of their group!

Even so, I've learned more about servant-leadership from Bruce than almost anyone I know. It has created a love and trust that I have rarely seen between a pastor and worship leader in a church. I have only twice in seven years asked Bruce to sing a particular song or asked him to replace one the congregation was being asked to sing. And one of those times Bruce said no. I accepted his no because I trust him. He knows better than I do what music is appropriate and he makes it easy for me to let him do his job. Our relationship has become so important that Bruce and his wife, Nikki, have become two of our very best friends. The power of servant-leadership, pastor to pastor, church to church, employer to employee, business to business, and government to government cannot be overstated. It is absolutely pro-found. It can change the world.

Bruce has found in his own sphere of influence the power of servant leadership. Not long ago, Hope built a state-of-the-art recording studio to record Church choirs and singer/songwriters that would never receive the attention or concern they deserved in recording their work. Having recorded numerous church choirs, international bands, and local recording artists, Hope sits right on the precipice of a new era in the recording industry. The sort of servant leadership that is a hallmark of Bruce's efforts will literally change the face of the Christian recording industry in the next five years. It's all the power of servant-leadership.

Jesus Christ had a lot to say about our responsibility as stewards of the gifts, talents, and abilities God has given us. We stand to be in a lot of trouble if we waste these valuable resources. He puts it this way,

> It's also like a man going off on an extended trip. He called his servants together and delegated responsibilities. To one he gave five thousand dollars, to another two thousand, to a third one thousand, depending on their abilities. Then he left. Right off, the first servant went to work and doubled his master's investment. The second did the same. But the man with the single thousand dug a hole and carefully buried his master's money.

> After a long absence, the master of those three servants came back and settled up with them. The one given five thousand dollars showed him how he had doubled his investment. His master commended him: "Good work! You did your job well. From now on be my partner."

> The servant with the two thousand showed how he also had doubled his master's investment. His master commended him: "Good work! You did your job well. From now on be my partner."

The servant given one thousand said, "Master, I know you have high standards and hate careless ways that you demand the best and make no allowances for error. I was afraid I might disappoint you, so I found a good hiding place and secured your money. Here it is, safe and sound down to the last cent."

The master was furious. "That's a terrible way to live! It's criminal to live cautiously like that! If you knew I was after the best, why did you do less than the least? The least you could have done would have been to invest the sum with the bankers, where at least I would have gotten a little interest.

"Take the thousand and give it to the one who risked the most. And get rid of this 'play-it-safe' who won't go out on a limb. Throw him out into utter darkness."

Matthew 25:14–30 The Message

Don't tell me I can't change the world. Don't tell me *you* can't change the world. Don't tell *yourself* you can't change the world. Ask that beautiful four-year-old girl if we're changing her world. You change the world one four-year-old at a time. You change the world one prostitute at a time. You change the world one adulterous life at a time, one stripper at a time. You change the world one egocentric leader at a time. You change the world one sick, poor, uneducated man, woman, boy, and girl at a time.

Okay, Let's Review:

1. What is one thing you can do today that can begin to make a difference in another person's life?

2. Is there a man, woman, boy, or girl you can make an appointment with today that will change *their* world?

3. Have you ever investigated soup kitchens, clothing closets, or help for the needy in your city where you could volunteer an hour a week?

4. This is almost your last chance.

Just do it.

ali's way: it could be your way, too

Ali was in the first grade when she first began her battle with cancer. As a first grader she had to grow up fast. Radical, painful, experimental treatments were necessary to keep her young body alive for what we all hoped would be many, many years.

I happened to be in Los Angeles a few days after she had begun an especially tough round of experimental treatments at Children's Hospital of Los Angeles and I thought it might mean something special to have her pastor from a world away drop in unannounced and unexpected to see her. I was right and that one visit created an immediate and lasting bond between Ali and me that never ended. Although I didn't even get to see her that first time in Los Angeles, she knew I was there and always remembered that simple act of kindness. From that moment forward, I was always Ali's pastor. Never mind that through the years she was sometimes active in the churches of her friends; in times of crises, Ali wanted to see me. I was honored. Always.

Thankfully, the cancer went into remission and even though it was always a constant part of her life, she lived life filled with gusto and passion and always eager optimism.

I saw Ali often at church, particularly when she was younger. I remember mornings at church when she would walk over to the place I was sitting before or after a service and give me a big hug. I was *her* pastor. She wrote books of poetry for me and she tried to live life with all of the joy, excitement, and fulfillment of every seven-year-old.

She was in the seventh grade when the cancer returned with a vengeance. More radical treatments, months at a time in the hospital, short, brave bouts then remission followed by another trip back to the hospital. I cherish the memory of talking to this little girl who was forced to grow up so fast, about heaven and hell. Her mother is one of my favorite friends and one of the most capable women I've ever known. She tells the story of Ali being confronted with this fear of where she was going when she died. What does one say to a child that has already experienced far more of the pain of life than I have in all of my years? Somehow our conversation brought some reassurance to her and so we waited. During the wait I met the most remarkable group of people I think I've ever known. They couldn't have been more diverse. There were liberals, conservatives, thinkers, feelers, believers and skeptics, and they were all in one group. They did not particularly go to the same church. Only one or two were from the church I call home. But what drew them all together were two dynamite little girls who were dying. Ali was one. She was mentoring the other. I found a twelve-year-old girl mentoring a little four-year-old girl named Emma Grace, both dying of cancer.

What drew the group together were these two precious little girls. The group was composed of the two mothers, two friends of the mothers, one of the primary cancer specialists who attended to these two girls and a young woman from the hospital who had fallen in love with these two little girls. About the time these girls faced the worst of their treatments, physically and emotionally, the cancer specialist, a brilliant man, and now a great friend to me, invited me to be a part of this very special small group. Now, you have to understand a little about the group. They met together and/or talked quite often when the girls were in the hospital, which was most of the time. But when the girls weren't in the hospital, they met by email. It was a loyal, strong, defiant, courageous, heroic group. They called themselves the ICO, the Inner Circle Only group. And I was not a part. Until one day Ray, my doctor friend whom I had met for the first time while visiting Ali, somewhat randomly invited me by email to join the group.

If you know Ray, nothing he does is really random. Inviting me to join the ICO was a calculated risk on his part. He was gambling that he could push this thing through. He sent me an email invitation to join the group and copied every other member of the group. Almost in unison, each one of them hit the "reply all" button and said almost the same thing, "We're not sure we want a preacher in the group. If he acts like most of the ministers we know, we don't have room for him. The last thing we need are his 'pat' answers." Of course, since it was sent to everyone, I got a copy, *and each of them knew it!* They simply didn't care. The trust that had been built among the members of that group was more important than the risk of one know-it-all preacher.

I wrote back, "I'm not sure I *want* to be in your group. If you're going to expect me to act like all the ministers you know, I'll opt out. Only if I can be myself will I come and I'm not all that sure you'll like what you find." I think my friend Ray sat in his home study and smirked while this dialogue transpired. Eventually we all called a truce and with fear and trepidation I timidly joined the ICO, and they cautiously if not reluctantly allowed me in.

The time I have spent with this group is some of the most cherished time in my life. I have often felt like I was walking on Holy Ground. The experience has been *that* sacred. This small group watched both of these little girls die. I was a part of both funerals, or celebrations of life, as we called them and they truly were. And I wept like a baby through both of them. I have never seen people ask harder questions, and face more pain, and love as deeply, and live with so much anguish, and work their way through it, than this group. Plodding along day after day, when these grieving moms could hardly breathe, and watching their pain was probably the most profound season of my life. I would find myself stepping into the pulpit on a routine weekend, barely able to preach knowing these mothers were in such pain. It made me ache for them.

If there is a place in the dictionary for a picture of a servant-leader, you would see a group photograph of the members of this group, the ICO, the Inner Circle Only group.

Nothing can soothe the ache in these mothers' hearts.

It's been a couple of years. We all wondered at the time how grief would mature. We all stay in touch. We still get together several times a year and we write each other, although it has become less and less frequent. But that time and that group has changed each of us forever. Pastors and doctors are not supposed to become so emotionally attached to their members/patients. They lose perspective. That's what we were taught. That was our formal education. And I can understand why. If I became that close to every person in crisis I would quickly lose my own ability to cope. But I wouldn't trade what I've learned from having gone through this heartbreaking experience with these stoic friends for anything in the world. The tragic reason for our gathering in the first place is becoming more of a gradual memory for some of us, although I'm positive both moms would tell you not a day goes by that they don't grieve over the loss of those precious little girls. But in the words of Henri Nouwen, they have become "wounded healers"[3] for others.

Why am I telling you this story? Because I don't want you to put this book down and say, "Well now, that was interesting." The thing I learned from Ali is not to give up, not to say it's too late. I learned how to live with hope. I learned how to believe God wasn't through with me yet. I learned how to be a wounded healer. I learned how to have fun even when the pain of life was almost unbearable. I learned that living life is a journey and you make of it what you will.

Why am I telling you this story? I want you to do something. *Do something!* I don't know any other way to say it. I want you to move outside your comfort zone and help somebody. I want you to realize that real faith is faith in action. It's not mere words. It's not something you exercise only for those in your tiny little circle. You exercise it because there are needs all around you that even extend to the very ends of the earth. And whether you go to the ends of the earth to reach out is not nearly as important as your *doing something!* There is plenty of time and room for you to spend the rest of your life living out your faith in practical ways.

Most of the world is sitting around waiting on somebody else. They're waiting for the rest of the world to join their little circle and then, and only then, will they reach out. And the little reaching they do, they do in their tiny circle—which isn't bad, it's just not good enough. Because we've proven by the condition of the world that the old way of doing it isn't working. Poverty isn't improving. Illiteracy isn't improving. Children dying from water-related diseases isn't improving. HIV/AIDS isn't improving. Spiritual darkness isn't improving. The world is not gradually teaching egocentric leaders how to be servant-leaders.

Rick Warren, in his book *The Purpose Driven Life,* has done a tremendous job of showing the average human being that he or she wasn't just put on earth to take up space. There is actually a purpose for each and every one of us.

Can we now agree to join hands with those who may not practice our particular brand of religion and go about changing our world? Can we now step out of the box? Can we leave our comfort zone, our tiny circles of conviction, and *just do something?* An entire world is waiting on us to put down the banner we wave and take up the cause that has kept us from changing the world.

You don't have to believe what your neighbor believes to love them. You can help them. You can encourage them. Maybe your neighbor is going through a divorce. Maybe your friend's daughter has cancer. Maybe your coworker has AIDS. Maybe your schoolmate is struggling with depression or loneliness.

Maybe you have a son or daughter who is addicted to alcohol or drugs and needs your tough love. Maybe they need somebody else's tough love. Make a phone call for help. If they won't accept it, accept it for yourself so that you too can become a wounded healer.

Maybe you're one of the lucky ones who aren't facing your own personal crises right this minute. What about Mexico, or Ecuador, or Kenya? Pick the developing country of your choice. Pick the needy person of your choice. Pick the cause of your choice. But for the sake of a lost and dying world, *do something!* Don't let the problems overwhelm you. You may not be able to change the world, but you can offer hope to a neighbor, encouragement to a sister, love to a coworker, aid to a distant hurting stranger. You may not be able to change the world, but you can change a little girl or boy's world. You may not be able to change the world, but you can change the world of your next-door neighbor. You may not be able to change the world, but you can change the world of the homeless man who finds his only hot meal at a soup kitchen that a group of a different faith sponsors. You can change the world of that young woman with HIV/AIDS who is literally dying and has no help for her little children.

Let's lay aside our differences and unite around a common cause. The massive problems of the world are not getting better; they're getting bigger. Pick one. Let's just do something and begin making the small differences that, gathered together, like many drops of water, become a Tsunami that can change the entire landscape of our world. It's up to you and it's up to me.

Okay, Let's Review:

1. Can you begin your own ICO?

2. Who do you know that you can extend a helping hand to *today?*

3. Is there *one* person you can call right now to offer love and support to?

4. What can you do right now that will change the way you live the rest of your life?

5. Do you know where the soup kitchens are in your city?

6. Can you volunteer? Do it today.

7. It's almost your last chance.

Just do it.

tales from the street

It was a little after two in the morning and I was riding with a lieutenant of one of the state's law enforcement agencies. Although I was raised in Memphis and know the city quite well, we were patrolling an area of the city that was foreign to me. Riding with cops is one of the most interesting and challenging parts of my world. We had been patrolling routinely for several hours in the middle of the night and all had been relatively quiet that night. All of a sudden, we saw an approaching car in a quiet neighborhood without any headlights. The lieutenant said, "That's not right. We better check that car out." He turned on his blue lights, made a U-turn, and raced to catch up to this out-of-the-ordinary car. When the driver saw the blue lights he took off and in a matter of seconds, the atmosphere changed from a casual conversation about family life in a cop's world to a gripping, highly charged, dangerous chase. It was like being on the television show, *Cops*, but without the video camera.

The car we were chasing made several sudden turns

and headed down a quiet residential street, pulled into a driveway and both passengers began to get out of the car. The lieutenant approached the driver and said, "Let me see your hands." The driver said, "What's the problem, man? I wasn't doing anything wrong." And what began as a very routine search suddenly became a physical confrontation. The passenger fled the scene and I found the lieutenant wrestling the driver to the ground. And I thought, "What's the chaplain supposed to do in this situation? I wasn't trained for this! Now there are people in the house that see us. Who knows if they're armed? Maybe the passenger who fled into the house will return with several of his family members and a stash of weapons. And in a few minutes, I'll be sorry I'm not wearing a bullet proof vest."

So in a fit of panic, I picked up the radio microphone in the car and said, "Dispatch! Officer down! Officer down!" At least that's what I think I said. To be honest, I was so scared I don't really remember exactly what I said. But the dispatcher immediately responded, "Please advise location, chaplain." So I looked at the address on the front of the house and said, "Fourteen-Fourteen..." I looked to my right and then to my left and realized I had no idea where we were. Not only did I not know the street, I didn't even recognize the neighborhood! Fortunately, the lieutenant had a portable radio and was able to call in the exact address. While I had idly been chatting through the night, he was vigilantly watching every street we passed and making mental notes of every potential problem we might face.

I have been fascinated with the subculture of law enforcement. After five years of working with cops, they have taught me a lot about the darker side of society while teaching me a lot about the world they live in. On the surface, it seems pretty different from our world. Every day a cop goes to work, he or she suits up, straps a gun around the waist (and often one somewhere else), and wonders if that day will be the day they have to take someone's life, or have their own threatened. In the back of their mind, they wonder if they'll be coming home at the end of their shift. Now, they would be quick to tell you that's no big deal. But you and I never ever get dressed in the morning with the thought stored in the back of our minds that maybe we'll lose our lives that day or have to take someone else's. Almost every car they pull over has a driver that didn't have but a couple of beers, wasn't driving over the speed limit, isn't out of control, has insurance although no evidence of it, or has a new set of tags at home they bought yesterday but just haven't had time to put on their vehicle yet. So cops tend to be skeptical of everything and everybody, and with very good reason.

I love working with cops. I think it's because they're more willing to announce their skepticism than hide behind it. In my role as a volunteer chaplain, if they don't like me, they just tell me. It's really very refreshing. I'm sure there are lots of people that don't like me that would just as soon I not know it.

Really, I find cops to be very much like the rest of us. They're just willing to say out loud what the rest of us are thinking on the inside. What do you think would happen if every pastor or priest were to stand in front of their flock and say, "You know, if I'm going to be completely honest with you, I need to tell you this: I sincerely believe everything I preach and teach with all my heart. But as sincerely as I believe it, surely I'm sincerely wrong about at least some of it. Because if I were completely right, it would mean that the rest of the world would have to be wrong. And there really is something bigger going on in the world than my own personal convictions. Moreover, I want to teach you all that I know, that I've studied and labored over, all that I've come to understand about God and humanity after my years of study and ministry. But at the end of the day, it's okay with me if you don't agree with me. It's okay if we agree to disagree. And I'm going to stop judging you for the places we disagree."

What if every person that had some sort of belief in God did the same thing? What if we all said, "You know, I don't hold the corner on truth. But one thing we ought to be able to agree on is that there is spiritual darkness, poor leadership, poverty, illness, and illiterate people in our backyard and all over the world. Why don't we set aside our differences and agree together to start changing our part of the world, whatever and wherever that may be?" What if we set aside the skepticism that causes us to distrust one another, that causes us to stand apart from each other, and joined hands? What if we started loving one another through the rough patches in life? What if we embraced people and their problems instead of turning our back in condemnation?

Do you think it's possible that we could make a difference? Is it possible that we could take a few small, simple steps that others might not even notice at first? Could we do something for someone today that would be tangible evidence of at least a feeble attempt at unconditional love? Instead of drawing our circle of conviction tightly and limiting those who can enter, could we turn the circle outward, agreeing to disagree on some things and uniting as an army that could gain enough force to impact the world?

No doubt it will be scary at times, and we won't know exactly where we are. I'm sure at times we will get disoriented because this all runs counter to our culture. I'm sure we'll have to wrestle with naysayers that will insist that their particular brand of religion or spirituality is the only possible way. I'm sure we will be heretics in the eyes of some and lunatics in the eyes of others. But in the process, we might just begin making a difference in the world. At first by the hundreds, maybe then by the thousands or even hundreds of thousands, and eventually by the millions. I'm simply not willing to say we can't make a difference. Let's just do it.

Okay, Let's Review:

1. Be honest. Are you going to put this book down and do nothing?

2. Is there someone you need to discuss this book with?

3. Will you take a sheet of paper and sketch out a game plan for how you plan to make your difference in the world?

4. What is step 1 for you?

Just do it.

endnotes

1. Brennan Manning, The Wisdom of Tenderness: What
    Happens When God's Fierce Mercy Transforms Our
    Lives, Harper Collins Publishing, Inc., 2002, p. 78.

2. Anup Shah, "Poverty Facts and Stats," last updated
    Friday, November 24, 2006.

3. Henri Nouwen, The Wounded Healer: Ministry in
    Contemporary Society, Darton, Longman & Todd,
    Ltd., 1994, p. 82.